GATL

The Seat Of Decision And Warfare

BY

Davidson Utsaghan

Published By

Kratos Publisher

GATE

Copyright ©2023 by DAVIDSON UTSAGHAN

Published by: Kratos Publisher

ACKNOWLEDGEMENT

Thanks be to God almighty for His faithfulness and mercies. Without Jesus Christ I am nothing . Glory to Him alone. I want to thank my beautiful wife Sarah for standing, believing and encouragement. To my two jewels love you lot and thanks for making me a proud father always. Thanks to all my family in Christ for your prayers and encouragement.

CONTENT

INTRODUCTION

When we look at the Bible, we often look at the place of the Gate as a prominent significant place in the Bible. There are many occasions in the Bible where 'GATE' is emphasised. In this book, we will explore the concept of 'GATE' as a place of entrance, the place of breakthrough, the seat of decision and authority, and the place of wealth and death.

Gate in the Scriptures symbolises a variety of essential things from ancient times. For example, Gates have been named after people, and we can see that concerning the twelve tribes of Israel, with the sons of Jacob having gates named after them.

So, in our understanding of gates, we are not just talking about physical gates; believers need to come to the realisation that when we talk about gates, we are talking about systems, spirits, and symbols that are there so that when we pray and war in the context of gates, we are talking about systems and certain things that stop us, or gives us access or something that God is unlocking. In effect, things that will trigger the manifestation of specific outcomes in the physical realm. Men will begin to open doors to you, and things will begin to work out for you in your favour. The answers to prayers we have been petitioning God for over a long period of time that has appeared unanswered will begin to manifest even after you have been contending, fasting, praying and asking God for solutions. Can these be the result of a Gate?

Sometimes a Gate can be a place of in-between, which is why we shall be exploring the concept of Gate as a place of decision in this book. We will see the symbolism of a gate being a place between your now and your next, hence the Gate being the place of decision. This could be why many people are stuck as they consider choosing between where they are and where they should be going. You can consider such persons stuck in the place of transition. You are in what I call the detained at the gate. We shall explore several scriptures as we continue breaking down the concept of Gate in this book. My prayer is to see your heart open and transform as we go, and I trust God to begin doing something supernatural in your life to help you break through the places of stagnation.

GATE AS ACCESS

A Gate can symbolise access or entrance, which is demonstrated in the scriptures. Matthew 16:18-19

And I say also unto thee, That thou art Peter, and upon this rock I will build my church; and the gates of Hell shall not prevail against it.

And I will give unto thee the keys of the kingdom of heaven: and whatsoever thou shalt bind on earth shall be bound in heaven: and whatsoever thou shalt loose on earth shall be loosed in heaven.

Jesus asked Peter a question that brought Peter into a place of access and in between his now and his next. I call this the Access and Key stage of his life, where a key is placed in his hands. If you are a believer, pastor, teacher, new Christian, leader, in an in-between stage of your life, there is a personal conviction and knowing when you

8

encounter God for yourself, that takes you to a higher dimension. That gives you access and also brings you into greater spheres of operation than when you are told about Him.

When Jesus came into the coasts of Caesarea Philippi, he asked his disciples, saying, Whom do men say that I the Son of man am?

And they said, Some *say that thou art* John the Baptist: some, Elias; and others, Jeremias, or one of the prophets.

He saith unto them, But whom say ye that I am?

And Simon Peter answered and said, Thou art the Christ, the Son of the living God.

Matthew 16:13-16

When Jesus asked His disciples whom do you say that I am, in Scripture, it is interesting to note Peter's answers as he opens the heart to what others say, but Jesus Asked them specifically Who do you say that I am? Peter says, "Thou art Christ, the Son of the Living God! Evidently, one can be in a place without knowing what to do or even the meaning of where they are, not recognising whom a person is, not understanding how a system functions, even though you have been operating within those systems all your life, which is a reflection of moving in circles, being confined within circles and cycles. The reality is that there is a gate present in such circumstances which restricts such a person to such circular limitations. **Gates restrict us from moving from one dimension to another.** There are city gates; a person can be in confinement and believe they have movement. Peter had his understanding shaped and defined by what he saw and heard in his surroundings, but when it came to his realisation of who Christ is? That gave him access to break out! Here we see the word of the Lord to Peter, saying that flesh and blood has not revealed this to you. Furthermore, we see Peter receiving the Keys, receiving this access and also, Jesus said upon this rock (Petros: means rock which is the Greek name peter) I will build my church, and the GATES of Hell shall not prevail! When we realise who Christ is, it breaks our mind out of confinement and frees us from spirits that have restricted us in places, breaking us out from things that have held us down for a long time.

Remember, when we are talking about Gates, we are referring to systems, spirits, ancient doors and foundational things that are present. As we read on, we see that Jesus told Peter that the gates of Hell shall not prevail. Peter's life is riddled with gates throughout his story. Two examples we will elaborate upon will be the Gate of beautiful in the book of acts and the angels opening the city's gates for him when he was liberated from prison.

Every believer must come to the revelation and realisation of knowing Christ intimately, leading to us breaking out of the systems, spirits and gates of Hell. Knowing Him breaks us from the manipulation and assignment from Hell that has come against us. God is calling us into the place of entering into Him. Entering into God gives us access to a greater dimension. Entering into God gives us entry into a global sphere and higher realms. So, it is not about looking for men or the understanding others carry, but understanding the revelation of God, who God is, exposes us to a life of revolution. It revolutionises our thinking as God begins to breathe his mind and spirit into us, and as we start to experience and know him, it expands our minds. It appears that the journey for the church is from strength to strength, from glory to glory and from height to height. I pray for you may the Lord's hand rest upon you, may everything that has clouded your mind and opened you up in a restricted way be broken and may he begin to give you access to a greater dimension and realm as you experience Him, may you begin to stand and walk and encounter and experience revolution as a result of the revelation in Jesus name.

As Peter came to the place of revelation, not to the ideology and information of men about Jesus Christ, He gave him access to a greater realm and dimension where the gates of Hell shall not prevail. He gave him the keys!

Keys – Access

Keys – Access

Keys – Access

Access represents entrances and portals. For example, the human body's five senses are entrances and portals like sight, smell, taste, hearing and touch. We don't want to expose our five senses to things that will confine us within systems. So I believe God will begin to do the miraculous and break us out into higher dimensions of Christ.

Talking about the gates of Hell, people have opened their eyes to false spirits, divination and different evil realms, and some call it the third eyes they have opened themselves to the gates of Hell.

When Hell unleashes sicknesses, pain, plague, and demonic things, things that keep us in cycles are released. The revelation of God closes the eyes of the ancient demonic gates, and it closes the eyes of Hell. It closes the entrance of Hell into your life because you have been exposed to a greater dimension of Christ.

GATES AS A PLACE OF BREAKTHROUGH

I get very excited when I talk about the Scripture regarding the place of breakthrough, Acts 12:8-11

And the angel said unto him, Gird thyself, and bind on thy sandals. And so he did. And he saith unto him, Cast thy garment about thee, and follow me.

And he went out, and followed him; and wist not that it was true which was done by the angel; but thought he saw a vision.

When they were past the first and the second ward, they came unto the iron gate that leadeth unto the city; which opened to them of his own accord: and they went out, and passed on through one street; and forthwith the angel departed from him.

Verse 10 shows us that Peter, after he had

passed the two guards, the angel took him to the city gate; I call that global influence, we can say the Gate of the city opened! There is a breakthrough that God is bringing for every one of us. I believe you are part of those to whom God will open the city gates. The influence is beyond the little things we have done in our prospective communities, but it is a global Gate and impact beyond your imagination. Until God opens the gates for you, no one can open them. Even though Peter was taken beyond the guards, certain things were still operating until the angel of the Lord opened the city gate. Once opened then, the angel left them. Here this God will open up the city Gates for you for the breakthrough.

Some of you have constantly been labouring, and every time you move or breakthrough, you have been restricted by city gates, systems, spirits or foundational systems. It seems you are moving around, but you get restricted when you get to that ancient Gate, the Gate that places everyone in confinement, that puts your family in captivity, I break it today, and I decree over your life that you will break forth out of this, your family will break forth out of this. Not by the hand of men but through the hands of His angels, God will break you out of the gates; a breakthrough is coming to your life, family and everything you are doing! I speak over your life and prophesy to you that your gates will no longer be held bound, that you will no longer be locked in-between the walls, you will no longer be locked in-between your city, God will give you access to whatever you believe God for! Expansion for breakthrough and elevation! I pray that the Almighty God will break you through in Jesus' name! I Love that as Peter went past the guards, I pray that God would open up the gates of the city in Jesus' name.

GATE A PLACE OF DECISION AND AUTHORITY

Her husband is known in the gates when he sits among the elders of the land.

Proverbs 31:23

Gates often is a place where decisions are made. Certain decisions will only come to pass due to the place of warfare at the Gate, the place of decision, the place of power, the place where you make reference, and the elders make decisions at the Gate! Gate is a system, spirit and warfare place. Often when we receive prophetic words about our futures, we get stuck not moving towards the declaration, but we get stuck in the transition between now and the next. Some people no longer know what to do when they get to the place in-between, therefore, find themselves lodging in the wrong camp and places. Although it sounds nice, it really is not nice. So when you arrive at the place of decision, be aware that you have arrived at the place of war for the future! You have arrived at the place to cry out for God's help!

I Pray that the Lord will help you, that God will stand with you as you read this book, and that you have come to the place of decision, the place called in-between, or the place where you feel stuck in life. I pray that the Lord will stand with you, that the Lord will lead you and send you helpers, that the Lord will protect you and take you through it, and may you come out through the Gate in Jesus' name.

We must understand the significance of gates in Scripture whilst looking at the beautiful Gate;

Act 3:1 Now Peter and John went up together into the temple at the hour of prayer, being the ninth hour.
Act 3:2 And a certain man lame from his mother's womb was carried, whom they laid daily at the Gate of the temple which is

called Beautiful, to ask alms of them that entered into the temple;

Act 3:3 Who seeing Peter and John about to go into the temple asked an alms.

Act 3:4 And Peter, fastening his eyes upon him with John, said, Look on us.

Act 3:5 And he gave heed unto them, expecting to receive something of them.

Act 3:6 Then Peter said, Silver and gold have I none; but such as I have give I thee: In the name of Jesus Christ of Nazareth rise up and walk.

Act 3:7 And he took him by the right hand, and lifted him up: and immediately his feet and ankle bones received strength.

Act 3:8 And he leaping up stood, and walked, and entered with them into the temple, walking, and leaping, and praising God.

Act 3:9 And all the people saw him walking and praising God

There seems to be an emphasis that at the 9th hour, Peter and John met this man at the Gate called beautiful. I often wonder why that Gate is called beautiful even though the man at the Gate had nothing with him; we can call beautiful. Have you ever been in a place where everything around you is beautiful? Or the news you are hearing is beautiful? Or it seems your family is beautiful, but you are called the black sheep or yellow sheep; whatever you are called that doesn't make you as beautiful. You might even be questioning God because you are about to give up because you are in a system that has restricted and conditioned you, or in a system where like the Gate of beautiful you are just sitting there. God will send helpers! In Jesus' name. The man at the Gate of beautiful often begged for money. When he saw Peter coming, he stretched out his hands and asked for money because that was his confinement; that is what kept him restricted to the Gate. His mindset was restricted to money just for today! Eat and live, no future, no plan; he was truly restricted. Maybe certain things are happening to you today, where there are no plans, no investments or generational wealth, no wealth for your children or plan for advancement. Everything you do now is let me work so I can pay my bills, I want to work so I can pay what is left over. **You are working to live rather than living to work.** This inflexion is a system where it seems you can't break through, stand up or move. There is an angel of the Lord that he is sending to you today to help you break through every restriction that might have been put your way. He is sending his hands to liberate you and turn you over to a greater dimension.

Peter did something unique, Peter said; Silver and gold have I none; but such as I have give I thee: In the name of Jesus Christ of Nazareth rise up and walk.

Peter took him from the place of despair, Peter a man God has said of him that the gates of Hell shall not prevail, pulled the man up and took him through the Gate of beautiful into the temple, into the place of beauty! Into the place where the man can now walk, and no longer needs to beg again! God will take you from being stuck and having no knowledge of the way forward, or economic uncertainty and even not knowing what you will eat, and God will help you break through and put you in the place of power, greatness and decision! Where you will be able to speak again! God will put your name in the mouth of people as they come to a realisation saying, is that not the man that sat there?

They used to look at you because of the gates. The place called Gate where you have been sitting, the system that's held you bound, the system that has held you behind, the system that has kept you in a plain, the system that's tied you, the system that has caused you not to grow, not to invest, not to become anything, not to open up your mouth that's shot you down. God is literally going to begin to take those cloaks off your life, and it's going to walk you through the doors again in the name of Jesus. Then now, you will rise and see the heart of God. The hand of God and the mind of God for you, your children, your family, and everything that God has called you to represent on earth, you are literally going to begin to see it. In the name of Jesus, I decree it. In the name of Jesus Christ.

LEPERS AT THE GATE

(2Ki 7:3) And there were four leprous men at the entering in of the Gate: and they said one to another, Why sit we here until we die?

(2Ki 7:4) If we say, We will enter into the city, then the famine is in the city, and we shall die there: and if we sit still here, we die also. Now therefore come, and let us fall unto the host of the Syrians: if they save us alive, we shall live; and if they kill us, we shall but die.

(2Ki 7:5) And they rose up in the twilight, to go unto the camp of the Syrians: and when they were come to the uttermost part of the camp of Syria, behold, there was no man there.

(2Ki 7:6) For the Lord had made the host of the Syrians to hear a noise of chariots, and a noise of horses, even the noise of a great host: and they said one to another, Lo, the King of Isra el hath hired against us the

kings of the Hittites, and the kings of the Egyptians, to come upon us.

(2Ki 7:7) Wherefore they arose and fled in the twilight, and left their tents, and their horses, and their asses, even the camp as it was, and fled for their life.

(2Ki 7:8) And when these lepers came to the uttermost part of the camp, they went into one tent, and did eat and drink, and carried thence silver, and gold, and raiment, and went and hid it; and came again, and entered into another tent, and carried thence also, and went and hid it.

We can see from the above Scripture that God did something quite significant in the lives of the lepers. After the declaration of the Man of God that by this time tomorrow, there will be a transition, shift and wealth transfer, God wrought extraordinary miracles through the lepers.

I believe there is a global wealth transfer occurring now, which I pray your life will be a part of, but as you can see, it took a gate to open. In order words, a decision was made at the Gate by the lepers, just like a decision was made at the Gate of beautiful. Such an excellent correlation between the Old and New Testament.

We can see from Scripture that the lepers said to themselves, "why do we sit here? Why are we at the gate? If we sit here continually, we will die", not knowing that the Prophet of God has spoken the word of the Lord, that will impact the Assyrian camp and cause an economic shift that will reinstate the selling of goods for shekels. Observationally, from Scripture, the word of God does not return to Him void. Therefore, when the word of the Lord has been spoken, you must run with it. When the lepers made their way to the camp, we notice from Scripture that the Assyrians took flight because, from their perspective, they heard the sound of war.

God will take you from a place where you desire death to a place of tremendous abundance, surplus, authority, increase, breakthrough, and power, just like He did for the lepers. This is where ABBA is taking you. He will lift you and your family from current circumstances into fulfilling His words. God will give what appears like foolish instruction to shift systems, spirits, gates and things that have been there or block you and restricts your access. I Pray that God will give you access and opportunity to bring you into a greater realm and higher dimension of surplus, increase and opportunity in the name of Jesus.

GATES OF JERUSALEM

Jer 17:19 Thus said the LORD unto me; Go and stand in the Gate of the children of the people, whereby the kings of Judah come in, and by the which they go out, and in all the gates of Jerusalem;

Jer 17:20 And say unto them, Hear ye the word of the LORD, ye kings of Judah, and all Judah, and all the inhabitants of Jerusalem, that enter in by these gates:

As evident within the above scriptures, the prophet speaks from the Gate, the entrance; there is an authority and understanding that in the midst of the system, we connect and plug into the systems of heaven and, in turn, reign on earth.

When Peter unlocked the revelation of the mind and heart of God, the person of Christ, keys were given to him to lose and bind within the heavens and earth.

And I will give unto thee the keys of the kingdom of heaven: and whatsoever thou shalt bind on earth shall be bound in heaven: and whatsoever thou shalt loose on earth shall be loosed in heaven.

Matthew 16:19

Access was given to him; when we plug into the systems and economy of heaven, and not the system of this world, it leads to a place of abundance and surplus and the prevailing of God's word. I Pray that as you begin to connect to the systems of heaven, you will begin to see an economic shift, spiritual shift, and shift in your health, home and everything concerning you in the name of Jesus.

The word of the Lord says in 3 John 1:2

Beloved, I wish above all things that thou mayest prosper and be in health, even as thy soul prospereth.

Peter had authority given to him, to bind and to lose. A place where the gates of Hell will not prevail over him, so I pray for you that authority is coming back to your mouth and life again, the ancient and demonic gates shall no longer stand in your life in the name of Jesus.

The Gate is also a place of decision and wealth; wealth and riches shall be in your house, as we can see with the examples of the lepers at the Gate in 1 kings, the place of wealth opened for them, the Gate of wealth opened for them, May the Gate of wealth open up for you and your family in Jesus name, you will no longer lack in Jesus name.

(Lam 5:14) The elders have ceased from the Gate, the young men from their musick.

My prayer is that you will not back down from the place of the Gate, decision and authority. This could be what Jacob understood when he wrestled with the angel of the Lord, and he came to a place of decision, a place between his now and his future and a place of war, wrestling and authority. Jacob wrestled and would not back down to the point that the angel said leave me. Let me go for the day is breaking, but Jacob will not, until the angel dislocated his hips and he began limping, but Jacob's name was changed from that of a trickster to Israel, a prince with God. Because of His encounter with God, this realisation led to the naming of bethel. That place became a portal, and a gate opened because of the wrestling and encounters in that place. A place of access, systems and authority opened up for Jacob, where his fears had to be faced, especially since His brother threatened to kill him upon any occasion of meeting him.

So if you have backed down from the place

of the Gate, I am encouraging and admonishing you to return to the place of the Gate, for it is the place to settle the scores. God will cause you to travail and pray like never before. He will help you to war and lead you to pray prayers of transformation, saying Lord change me and help me to battle.

I pray the Lord will break every cloud that has held you down, restricted you, or placed you in bondage, so you can advance to your next level and the place where God is calling you. As God is causing us to prevail, the gates of Hell (hades) will not prevail, and the gates of witchcraft and manipulation will not prevail over your life in Jesus' name.

A gate is not a fictional reality, but gates represent; systems, spirits, entities, principalities and powers that have stood against you. It takes the revelation of Christ to dismantle the gates of Hell.

When we speak about gates, we are also speaking about ancient gates that will obey God's voice and the Father's cry.

According to Scripture.

(Psa 24:9) Lift up your heads, O ye gates; even lift them up, ye everlasting doors; and the King of glory shall come in.

(Psa 24:10) Who is this King of glory? The LORD of hosts, he is the King of glory. Selah.

The King of glory will open up every closed Gate that has been closed in your life in Jesus' name.

As Peter moved from being between guards to the gates being opened for him, we are praying that every Gate that has been shut and has stood in your way will begin to lift up their head because the King of glory is coming up again in the name of Jesus.

The Scripture says;

(Psa 118:19) Open to me the gates of righteousness: I will go into them, and I will praise the LORD:

May the Gate of righteousness be opened to you in Jesus Christ's name.

The demonic gates, systems, portals and entities will not prevail, especially when you are ready for change. The change will only come to those who say, "I am tired of this", and those who have had enough. Change doesn't happen to those who sit and do nothing, those that prefer the status quo. Change only comes to those who have an attitude about doing something to alter their current circumstances.

It is time for you to fight, it is time for you to go for it, and it is time for you to war for change.

(Gen 32:24) And Jacob was left alone; and there wrestled a man with him until the breaking of the day.

We can see that Jacob wrestled for change, and the gates of heaven opened.

May the city gate open to you in Jesus name.

Iron Gates

(Act 12:10) When they had passed the first and the second guard, they came to the iron gate leading into the city. It opened for them of its own accord, and they went out and went along one street, and immediately the angel left him.

There are iron gates that lead to cities, I pray that the Lord will war for you and the Lord will stand with you. Every iron gate, and strong barrier are placed there to confine and restrict things in certain places.

As the Lord opens things for you, be attentive with your ears.

(Act 12:14) Recognising Peter's voice, in her joy she did not open the Gate but ran in and reported that Peter was standing at the Gate.

(Act 12:15) They said to her, "You are out of

your mind." But she kept insisting that it was so, and they kept saying, "It is his angel!"

(Act 12:16) But Peter continued knocking, and when they opened, they saw him and were amazed.

We can see in this Scripture that the girl recognised the voice. Without a doubt, the people were crying and praying, and when it was time to break out and through and receive an answer to their prayers, they couldn't but the girl's recognition prevailed.

Peter left one Gate and was now standing at another gate so he could embrace his people.

(Isa 60:11) Your gates shall be open continually; day and night they shall not be shut, that people may bring to you the wealth of the nations, with their kings led in procession.

God will open everything that has limited your access, money, wealth, investment, and family. Your Gate will open continually in Jesus' name, not just open and close again. Just as the word of the Lord in Isaiah.

Continually means never-ending; always, it is not stop-and-go or intermittent. It is not one step forward and four steps backwards.

The emphasis is not that the gates will be open during the day alone, but they will be opened day and night.

Reiterating the point, Gate is the place of wealth, riches, advancement, authority and decision.

(Gen 22:17) I will surely bless you, and I will surely multiply your offspring as the stars of heaven and as the sand that is on the seashore. And your offspring shall possess the Gate of his enemies,

Do you see what the lepers did in 2 Kings 7? Remember, these are not just barricades; they are systems, wealth, riches, promises and things God has put on that ancient path. These things can either be demonic or Godly, and there are storehouses; a gate can be like a storehouse. I pray that the Lord will help us step and possess the Gate of our enemies in Jesus' name.

We are in a time of the most outstanding wealth transfer, and the Bible says the wealth of the wicked is laid for the righteous. There is a transfer coming to the body of Christ; let us position ourselves for a mega that God is bringing.

So Gate is an entrance into the city or

market place, its an access, it is time for heaven's agenda to begin to operate down here on earth. God is doing something so significant in His church. We have to begin to rise up and begin to possess what is ours. He wants us to rise, and all the things he has given us, He will put them in our hands again, every contention, fight, warfare, foundational spirit and ancient Gate that is standing against us, demonic gate or system gate, territorial Gate will not prevail in Jesus name.

It is also a place of death; one place must be killed for the other place to rise again. We saw this in the life of Jacob, and he had to be transformed. So, God is doing a transforming work in our lives, and He is causing us to walk in a greater dimension. He is opening us to a greater place. He is breaking through iron doors for us; things will shift quickly because God is causing his people to rise up, men who can pray, men who can war, men who say, Lord, I will not sit at this Gate that looks beautiful, begging. I will not stay here, I am contending for more, a greater dimension, and an increase. God will place kingdom, wealth and purpose into your hands in Jesus' name.

GATES OF INFLUENCE

As we talk about Gate, it represents the place in the seat of influence of authority and power. In the bible, Gate is mentioned 275 times, while the plural description Gates is mentioned 144 times.

Understanding gates from a warfare and breakthrough perspective, we see clearly that there is a contention, a fight, and a war for gates. This is why intercessors and watchmen must understand that the protection of the gates is mandatory.

It seems there are many intercessors and watchmen within the body of Christ that have left the Gate. We have left our posts and pursuing so much in the world that we have been distracted.

In the media, family, religion, education, business, entertainment and government, the enemy sits in these spheres because that is the place of authority and influence.

We have left the Gate where decisions are made, people are seating, making decisions about us whom should not be making them.

It is now time for us to rise up, because we have left our position and the place of our authority. There is suffering in the family sphere. That is why we are getting things introduced into homes because we have left our gates open and are no longer interested in the place of warfare within the family. Where they are now telling us it's man and man or woman and woman, all sorts of gender has been introduced.

In the sphere of religion, people are engaging in cultism, voodoo and witchcraft because the seat has been left vacant due to our distraction and lack of focus.

In our educational system, perversion is being taught to our children, bringing such things into our schools. Why are such things happening? It is because there is a fight for the seat.

In the media sphere, even with Disney, you can see all these demonic things are in place now where the place of decision and authority are doing all they can to win our kids, emotions and minds over. We must now capture that revelation that peter caught and received keys as he did. We must begin to reclaim our keys, our dominion and our place of influence.

In the entertainment sphere, we see the impact of music within the home and the generation because of the kind of people sitting at that Gate.

In the business and commerce sphere, we have sadly not been taught well as believers, but it is now high time for us to understand this space.

In the government sphere, we have sadly named the government demonic and corrupt, and no believers want to sit at that

Gate or engage at that level and hence allow others to sit at that Gate. It is now time to rise up, intercessors, warriors and prayer warriors and come back to take our spheres.

TWELVE GATES TWELVE TRIBES

The importance of Gates cannot be over-emphasised; if the Bible mentions Gate 275 times and 144 times in the plural form, then we must pay attention.

In Nehemiah, we see the importance of rebuilding the gates, and there were twelve gates mentioned in Nehemiah. The sheep gate, fish gate, valley gate, old Gate, dung Gate, fountain gate, water gate, horse gate, east Gate, prison gate, Ephraim gate, and Miphkad gate. All these Gates symbolise power where we believers must begin to rise up.

The rebuilding of the wall and the twelve gates within it is a symbol of what God is restoring. I believe God is restoring the church back to its place of authority. These twelve gates represent the structure that will bring us back to a place of decision that impacts all the global spheres. The twelve Gate also represented the 12 tribes.

The Sheep Gate: is a symbol for souls that are getting saved, repentance and new birth.

*(Neh 3:1) Then Eliashib the high priest rose up with his brothers the priests, and they built the **Sheep Gate**. They consecrated it and set its doors. They consecrated it as far as the Tower of the Hundred, as far as the Tower of Hananel.*

We can see that Jesus Christ became the door, and He is calling us, the sheep, to come in. This gives us insight into the mind of God as He brings us to alignment again. The Father is restoring the sheep gate in these times, the wolves has been coming to attempt destroying the sheep, just like the devil is a wolf and roaring lion. Whilst the sheep represents the disciples and children of God. God is in these times rebuilding and given access to the sheep in the context of discipleship and bringing back the children of God as we can see in scripture.

(Joh 10:27) My sheep hear my voice, and I know them, and they follow me:

The sheep gate is being restored and will open up a place where his disciples will be able to hear the voice of ABBA and the Lord Jesus Christ. The sheep are being called not the goats, we must note the difference between the sheep and the goats. Goats are rebellious when they are called, whilst when sheep are called they follow. The seat of discipleship is being rebuilt now, and the devil will not be able to snatch the sheep out of the hands of God.

The Fish Gate: the parallel of this Gate can be seen in the life of Peter when Jesus said to him follow me, and I will make you a fisher of men. The fish Gate represents Evangelism.

(Mat 4:19) And he saith unto them, Follow me, and I will make you fishers of men.

The time for recycling members of various churches is coming to an end, as God will be bringing in new souls saved in evangelism, so there is a restoration of the evangelism gate which is the fish gate. Opportunities for souls to be saved. I pray the Lord will begin to empower us again as unbelievers begin to flock into the house of the Father to find refuge. Not to be judged in the house of God, the phenomenon where unbelievers after they are saved and come into the church are expected to behave as believers immediately will come to an end as the Fish Gate is getting restored within the house of God. The fight for the fish gate will be won as we take a stand to see souls saved.

The Old Gate: discusses bringing us back to foundational truths and ancient realities. This gate is a stronghold and also represents ancient gate as we can see in scripture;

(Psa 24:9) Lift up your heads, O gates! And lift them up, O ancient doors, that the King of glory may come in.

The ancient doors and gates are opening for the king Jesus is coming in as we dismantle strongholds of the past and rebuild the new God is bringing in Jesus name.

The Valley Gate: I enjoy speaking about the valley experience, where we are humbled and a place where we come to brokenness,

(Luk 3:5) Every valley shall be filled, and every mountain and hill shall be made low,

and the crooked shall become straight, and the rough places shall become level ways,

The Scripture demonstrates that when we humble ourselves, God will exalt us.

The Dung Gate: the dung gate represents a wasteful place where things are thrown and where dung is excreted. This Gate is where we deal with demonic things and uncleanness.

The Fountain Gate: This represents a place of bath, cleansing, cleaning, purity, and holiness.

(Zec 13:1) In that day there shall be a fountain opened to the house of David and to the inhabitants of Jerusalem for sin and for uncleanness.

The Horse Gate: represents power, strength and warfare; we can see this in

Nehemiah.

The Water Gate: Here is where we talk about baptism; the Bible says the water and the word wash us.

God is bringing back purity through the water Gate, also the Spirit of God is like rivers of water that washes over us and purifies us. This is the expression as the water breaks the Spirit of God breaks out on us.

So we are washed by the water and by the Word according to scriptures;

(Eph 5:26) that he might sanctify her, having cleansed her by the washing of water with the word,

(Eph 5:27) so that he might present the church to himself in splendor, without spot or wrinkle or any such thing, that she might be holy and without blemish.

Nehemiah's action in restoring the wall and gates is quite significant in bringing the people of God back to the place of power, warfare, decision, ruling, and authority and a place where we get back our seats.

The East Gate: represents a place from where the sun rises. This displays the dominion and the glory of the Lord. Arise and shine for your light, and the Lord's glory has risen upon you.

(Eze 43:1) Then he led me to the gate, the gate facing east.

(Eze 43:2) And behold, the glory of the God of Israel was coming from the east. And the sound of his coming was like the sound of many waters, and the earth shone with his glory.

(Eze 43:3) And the vision I saw was just like the vision that I had seen when he came to destroy the city, and just like the vision that

I had seen by the Chebar canal. And I fell on my face.

(Eze 43:4) As the glory of the LORD entered the temple by the gate facing east,

There is a rising up that the east symbolises just as the sun rises from the east. As we begin to take dominion and shine as sons of God.

The Ephraim Gate: this represents double because Ephraim represents fruitfulness, being productive, a gate of fruitfulness and abundance.

God is restoring us at the gates.

Joseph was in the land of Egypt, Egypt is a symbol of draught, pain and hardship. In Egypt God favoured Joseph, therefore Joseph names his son Ephraim, which means fruitfulness. So God is restoring the Gate of fruitfulness in Jesus name!

(Gen 41:52) And the name of the second called he Ephraim: For God hath caused me to be fruitful in the land of my affliction.

Whilst there is darkness on the earth the believers will begin to rise up and shine as lights, millionaires will rise up and be fruitful from within the body of Christ in Jesus name, because the gate of Ephraim is being restored in this time.

The Miphkad Gate: this represents rewards and punishment. This is the Gate of reward. It represents assignment; appointment also means a commander.

There is a difference between getting busy and fulfilling our assignment and purpose as we see in Nehemiah.

The word Miphkad in Hebrew means assignment.

God is bringing a restoration of assignment in the life of believers as they will no longer be running around working without understanding their assignment. May we walk in our assignment. Your assignment is your purpose on earth. I pray that we will take the gate of assignment, the gate of Miphkad, and not just fulfilling other people's dream, or helping other people's assignment and businesses whilst we are not fulfilling ours. So God will restore the Gate of assignment in Jesus name.

The Prison Gate; represents a place of reflection and rethinking up to the point of becoming like paul, a prisoner of the Lord, having a clear understanding of the mind and will of God.

God is restoring the church back into the place of influence within the family, education, business and commerce, sports, government and religion where we rise up back to the place of authority.

So I pray that our Gate shall continually be open in Jesus' name.

PRAYERS

I want you to decree and declare. Say, Father, today I contend with every Gate, oh God, that has stood between me and my next. I take authority over every family gate, every religious Gate, educational gate, media gate, entertainment gate, business gate, and government gate, and take access today to the next and I prevail today. Over these gates, in the name of Jesus, Father, I cried to thee that I would not be found in the beautiful Gate and not crossed over to the place of beauty. So today, I access authority. Father, oh God, that you gave to Peter. Whatsoever we bind on Earth shall be bound in heaven. So not today, I decree that I am an overcomer. No gates shall stand against my life, against my family. In the name of Jesus, Father, I decree today I stand. I break every force to take authority over powers, principalities against my life, that content against me.

The Gate of Hell shall not prevail against me, shall not prevail against my assignment, shall not prevail against my ministry, shall not prevail against my business in the name of Jesus, and I come against every demonic Gate, every iron gate, every iron gate stopping me. Father, I break. I shall not be local-bound but global-bound. I decree and declare that my spares are open, and my spheres are expanded in Jesus' name. Amen.

DECLARATION PRAYERS

Wealth gates

I decree and declare oh wealth gate, open for me, my family and my business. For the wealth of the wicked is laid up for the righteous, no longer shall I strive, sit back and wealth pass me. Oh my hands capture wealth like never before. Oh wealth gate open for my family, oh wealth gate open for me. Lord you said, according to your word wealth an riches shall be in my house, so the gate of wealth and riches shall be open for me. I walk into wealth like never before, generational wealth open for me, my family and my children.

Iron gates

I declare no longer shall my life be held back by iron gate, as the iron gate was open for peter; I decree and declare, my life shall not be held back by iron gates. Generational iron gates, ancestral iron gates, ancient iron gates that has kept me in obscurity, that has kept me in stagnation, I break that gate today! So Lord, I decree and declare that iron gate will not keep me bound, that iron gate will not hold be back, so iron gate open for me into a global ministry, into a global business, into a global adventure, open for me internationally, iron gate open! I decree and declare that my life will not be bound. In the name of Jesus.

Fish Gate

I decree and declare! Oh fish gate open for me, oh fish gate let the wealth begin to flow, let the stock begin to come in. As the coin was taken out of the mouth of the fish, oh fish gate open, open on your own accord, bring wealth unto me and my family

East Gate

Oh east Gate as the sun rises from the east I decree that my life will rise up, oh east gate open for me, let there be an arising concerning my life, every stagnation from the past, oh east gate open for me and let there be supernatural favour in the name of Jesus.

Marriage Gate

Marriage Gate open for me, no longer shall I be stranded concerning marriage and things concerning my family, we ask that the marriage gate be opened for us, let the home become the home of unity, oneness and orderliness, let wealth and riches flow into our home. No longer shall it be heard that the singles are not getting married in Jesus name. Father let there be favour, marriage gate open for us. Family gate open for us, in the name of Jesus Christ. We decree and declare that the goodness of the Father shall rest upon our homes again in the name of Jesus Christ. We ask that every thing that has held us bound previously be taking out of the way in the name of Jesus Christ.

Every gate that has kept us in limitation, it is a new day of advancement, greatness, power, increase and strength. We say the seat gate that has been placed back, Lord we take our seat back today, the position and place you have called us. Father we thank you because you have given it to us in Jesus name. Amen

Gate

Printed in Great Britain
by Amazon

17917015R00038